MY FIRST
ANIMAL ABC

Du même auteur

Les mots anglais du français (et autres mots transparents),
Autoédition, 2018, ISBN : 9781983140358

Back to English – Revoir les bases, renouer avec l'anglais,
Editions Ellipses, 2020, ISBN : 9782340037540

MY FIRST ANIMAL ABC

Thomas GAUTHIER

 Download the audio tracks from
www.msieurthomas.com

Loi n°49-956 du 16 juillet 1949 sur les publications destinées à la jeunesse, modifiée par la loi n°2011-525 du 17 mai 2011.

Édition : BoD – Books on Demand,
12/14 rond-point des Champs-Élysées, 75008 Paris
Impression : BoD - Books on Demand, Norderstedt, Allemagne

© 2022 Thomas Gauthier
www.msieurthomas.com

Illustrations : www.pixabay.com
sauf le numbat : Rawpixel Ltd - Numbat shade drawing

Pistes audio enregistrées au Sweet Beats Studio
www.sweetbeatsstudio.fr

ISBN – 978-2-32241-177-1
Dépôt légal: Février 2022

"Repetition is the mother of all learning."

Standard set of phonetic symbols for English and examples

Source : https://www.phon.ucl.ac.uk/home/wells/phoneticsymbolsforenglish.htm

Consonants

/p/	*pen, copy, happen*
/b/	*back, baby, job*
/t/	*tea, tight, button*
/d/	*day, ladder, odd*
/k/	*key, clock, school*
/g/	*get, giggle, ghost*
/tʃ/	*church, match, nature*
/dʒ/	*judge, age, soldier*
/f/	*fat, coffee, rough, photo*
/v/	*view, heavy, move*
/θ/	*thing, author, path*
/ð/	*this, other, smooth*
/s/	*soon, cease, sister*
/z/	*zero, music, roses, buzz*
/ʃ/	*ship, sure, national*
/ʒ/	*pleasure, vision*
/h/	*hot, whole, ahead*
/m/	*more, hammer, sum*
/n/	*nice, know, funny, sun*
/ŋ/	*ring, anger, thanks, sung*
/l/	*light, valley, feel*
/r/	*right, wrong, sorry, arrange*
/j/	*yet, use, beauty, few*
/w/	*wet, one, when, queen*

Vowels

/ɪ/	*kit, bid, hymn, minute*
/e/	*dress, bed, head, many*
/æ/	*trap, bad*
/ɒ/	*lot, odd, wash*
/ʌ/	*strut, mud, love, blood*
/ʊ/	*foot, good, put*
/iː/	*fleece, sea, machine*
/eɪ/	*face, day, break*
/aɪ/	*price, high, try*
/ɔɪ/	*choice, boy*
/uː/	*goose, two, blue, group*
/əʊ/	*goat, show, no*
/aʊ/	*mouth, now*
/ɪə/	*near, here, weary*
/eə/	*square. fair, various*
/ɑː/	*start, father*
/ɔː/	*thought, law, north, war*
/ʊə/	*poor, jury, cure*
/ɜː/	*nurse, stir, learn, refer*
/ə/	*about, common, standard*
/i/	*happy, radiate. glorious*
/u/	*thank you, influence, situation*
/n̩/	*suddenly, cotton*
/l̩/	*middle, metal*
ˈ	*(stress mark)*

A a

/eɪ/

Alfred

the **a**lligator

Alfred

/ˈælfrəd /

A.L.F.R.E.D

alligator

/ˈælɪɡeɪtər/

A.L.L.I.G.A.T.O.R

B b

/biː/

Benny

the **b**ear

Benny

/ˈbɛni/

B.E.N.N.Y

bear

/beəʳ/

B.E.A.R

C c

/siː/

Claudia

the **c**amel

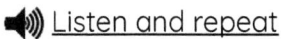

Claudia

/ˈklɔːdɪə/

C.L.A.U.D.I.A

camel

/ˈkæməl/

C.A.M.E.L

D d

/diː/

Derek

the **d**ormouse

Derek

/ˈdɛrɪk/

D.E.R.E.K

dormouse

/ˈdɔːmaʊs/

D.O.R.M.O.U.S.E

E e

/iː/

Eddy

the **e**lephant

Eddy

/ˈɛdi/

E.D.D.Y

elephant

/ˈɛlɪfənt/

E.L.E.P.H.A.N.T

F f

/ɛf/

Fiona

the **f**rog

Fiona

/fiˈoʊnə/

F.I.O.N.A

frog

/frɒg/

F.R.O.G

G g

/dʒiː/

Gina

the **g**oat

Gina

/ˈʤiːnə/

G.I.N.A

goat

/gəʊt/

G.O.A.T

H h

/eɪʧ/

Hector

the **h**ippo

Hector

/ˈhɛktə/

H.E.C.T.O.R

hippo

/ˈhɪpəʊ/

H.I.P.P.O

I i

/aɪ/

Irene

the **i**guana

Irene

/ˈaɪriːn/

I.R.E.N.E

iguana

/ɪˈgwɑːnə/

I.G.U.A.N.A

J j

/ʤeɪ/

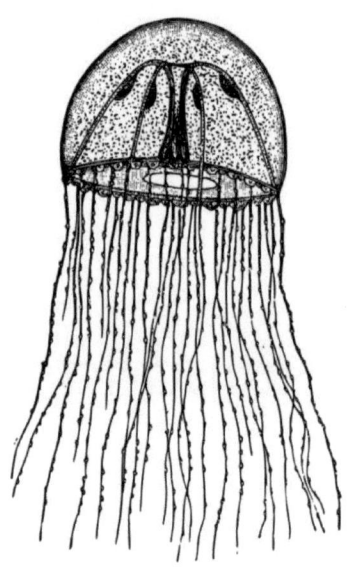

Jenny

the **j**ellyfish

Jenny

/ˈʤɛni/

J.E.N.N.Y

jellyfish

/ˈʤɛlɪfɪʃ/

J.E.L.L.Y.F.I.S.H

K k

/keɪ/

Kim

the **k**angaroo

Kim

/kɪm/

K.I.M

kangaroo

/ˌkæŋɡəˈruː/

K.A.N.G.A.R.O.O

L l

/ɛl/

Louis

the **l**lama

Louis

/ˈluːɪs/

L.O.U.I.S

llama

/ˈlɑːmə/

L.L.A.M.A

M m

/ɛm/

Maurice

the **m**oose

Maurice

/ˈmɒrɪs/

M.A.U.R.I.C.E

moose

/muːs/

M.O.O.S.E

N n

/ɛn/

Neil

the **n**umbat

Neil

/niːl/

N.E.I.L

numbat

/ˈnʌmbət/

N.U.M.B.A.T

O o

/əʊ/

Olga

the **o**tter

Olga

/ˈɒlgə/

O.L.G.A

otter

/ˈɒtə/

O.T.T.E.R

P p

/piː/

Peter

the **p**latypus

Peter

/ˈpiːtə/

P.E.T.E.R

platypus

/ˈplætɪpəs/

P.L.A.T.Y.P.U.S

Q q

/kjuː/

Queenie

the **q**uail

Queenie

/ˈkwiːni/

Q.U.E.E.N.I.E

quail

/kweɪl/

Q.U.A.I.L

R r

/aː/ - / ar/

Ricky

the **r**hino

Ricky

/ˈrɪkiː/

R.I.C.K.Y

rhino

/ˈraɪnəʊ/

R.H.I.N.O

S s

/ɛs/

Suzy

the **s**loth

Suzy

/ˈsuːzi/

S.U.Z.Y

sloth

/sləʊθ/

S.L.O.T.H

T t

/ti :/

Travis

the **t**apir

Travis

/ˈtrævɪs/

T.R.A.V.I.S

tapir

/ˈteɪpə/

T.A.P.I.R

U u

/juː/

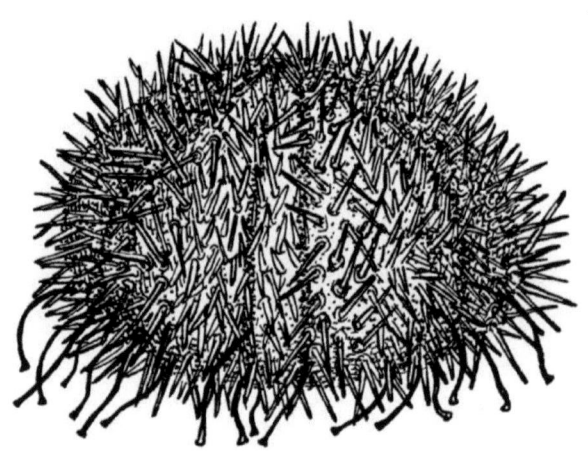

Ursula

the **u**rchin

Ursula

/ˈɜrsələ/

U.R.S.U.L.A

urchin

/ˈɜːtʃɪn/

U.R.C.H.I.N

V v

/viː/

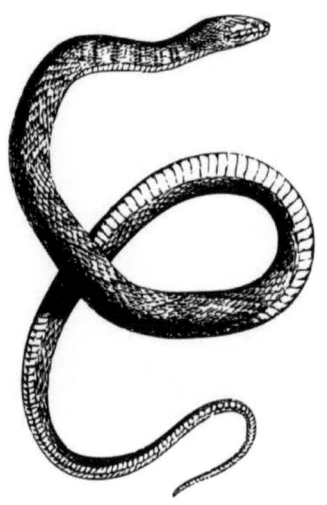

Veronica

the **v**iper

Veronica

/vɪˈrɒnɪkə/

V.E.R.O.N.I.C.A

viper

/ˈvaɪpə/

V.I.P.E.R

W w

/ˈdʌbljuː/

Willy

the **w**ombat

Willy

/ˈwɪli /

W.I.L.L.Y

wombat

/ˈwɒmbət/

W.O.M.B.A.T

/ɛks/

Xena

the lyn**x**

Xena

/ˈziːnə/

X.E.N.A

lynx

/lɪŋks/

L.Y.N.X

Y y

/waɪ/

Yanis

the **y**ak

Yanis

/ˈjænəs/

Y.A.N.I.S

yak

/jæk/

Y.A.K

Z z

/zɛd/ - /zi:/

Zoe

the **z**ebra

Zoe

/ˈzəʊi/

Z.O.E

zebra

/ˈziːbrə/

Z.E.B.R.A

ACTIVITIES

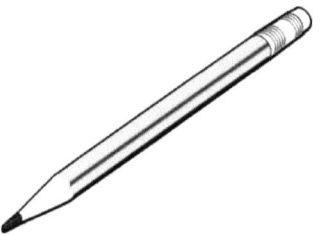

▶ <u>What's the first letter?</u> (1)

1. _ak

2. _amel

3. _angaroo

4. _apir

5. _ear

6. _ebra

▶ <u>What's the first letter?</u> (2)

1. _ellyfish

2. _guana

3. _hino

4. _iper

5. _ippo

6. _lama

► <u>What's the first letter?</u> (3)

1. _latypus

2. _lephant

3. _lligator

4. _loth

5. _oat

6. _ombat

►What's the first letter? (4)

1. _oose

2. _ormouse

3. _rchin

4. _rog

5. _tter

6. _uail

7. _umbat

8. _ynx

▶ <u>Unscramble the letters</u> (1)

1. g-i-l-a-l-o-r-t-a

   _ _ _ _ _ _ _ _ _

2. b-a-e-r-z

   _ _ _ _ _

3. m-a-b-o-t-w

   _ _ _ _ _ _

4. a-k-y

   _ _ _

5. e-i-p-r-v

   _ _ _ _ _

6. m-l-e-c-a

   _ _ _ _ _

► <u>Unscramble the letters</u> (2)

1. m-l-l-a-a

 _ _ _ _ _

2. p-p-o-i-h

 _ _ _ _ _

3. r-e-b-a

 _ _ _ _

4. g-r-f-o

 _ _ _ _

5. n-r-o-i-h

 _ _ _ _ _

6. o-n-k-r-a-g-a-o

 _ _ _ _ _ _ _ _

1. s-o-m-o-e

 _ _ _ _ _

2. t-o-g-a

 _ _ _ _

3. t-p-n-l-h-e-e-a

 _ _ _ _ _ _ _ _

4. t-r-p-i-a

 _ _ _ _ _

5. t-s-o-l-h

 _ _ _ _ _

6. t-t-r-o-e

 _ _ _ _ _

►<u>Unscramble the letters</u> (4)

1. n-i-g-u-a-a

   _ _ _ _ _ _

2. l-u-q-i-a

   _ _ _ _ _

3. r-n-i-h-c-u

   _ _ _ _ _ _

4. s-r-o-u-o-m-e-d

   _ _ _ _ _ _ _ _

5. u-t-n-m-a-b

   _ _ _ _ _ _

6. y-s-l-l-j-i-h-f-e

   _ _ _ _ _ _ _ _ _

7. u-t-s-p-y-p-l-a

   _ _ _ _ _ _ _ _

8. y-x-n-l

   _ _ _ _

69

►Connect the name to the animal (1)

1. ˈmɒrɪs   •   •   A. ˈdʒɛlɪfɪʃ

2. vɪˈrɒnɪkə   •   •   B. ˈhɪpəʊ

3. ˈkwiːni   •   •   C. ˈvaɪpə

4. ˈdɛrɪk   •   •   D. ˈlɑːmə

5. ˈdʒɛni   •   •   E. ˈkæməl

6. ˈjænəs   •   •   F. ˈteɪpə

7. ˈaɪriːn   •   •   G. lɪŋks

8. ˈklɔːdɪə   •   •   H. muːs

9. ˈhɛktə   •   •   I. jæk

10. ˈrɪkiː   •   •   J. ɪˈgwɑːnə

11. ˈluːɪs   •   •   K. kweɪl

12. ˈtrævɪs   •   •   L. ˈraɪnəʊ

13. ˈziːnə   •   •   M. ˈdɔːmaʊs

►Connect the name to the animal (2)

1. kɪm   •   • A. ˈɛlɪfənt

2. ˈpiːtə   •   • B. gəʊt

3. ˈwɪli   •   • C. ˈɒtə

4. ˈsuːzi   •   • D. ˈziːbrə

5. ˈælfrəd   •   • E. ˈɜːʧɪn

6. niːl   •   • F. ˈplætɪpəs

7. ˈʤiːnə   •   • G. beəʳ

8. ˈzəʊi   •   • H. frɒg

9. ˈbɛni   •   • I. ˌkæŋgəˈruː

10. ˈɛdi   •   • J. sləʊθ

11. fiˈoʊnə   •   • K. ˈwɒmbət

12. ˈɒlgə   •   • L. ˈnʌmbət

13. ˈɜːsələ   •   • M. ˈælɪgeɪtəʳ

🔊 Listen and write the number next to the corresponding animal (1)

73

🔊 Listen and write the number next to the corresponding animal (2)

▶Who are they?

1.

This is _____ the _____.

2.

This is _____ the _____.

3.

This is _____ the _____.

4.

This is _____ the _____.

5.

This is _____ the _____.

6.

This is _____ the _____.

7.

This is _____ the _____.

8.

This is _____ the _____.

9.

This is _____ the _____.

10.

This is _____ the _____.

11.

This is _____ the _____.

12.

This is _____ the _____.

13.

This is _____ the _____.

14.

This is _____ the _____.

15.

This is _____ the _____.

16.

This is _____ the _____.

17.

This is _____ the _____.

18.

This is _____ the _____.

19.

This is _____ the _____.

20.

This is _____ the _____.

21.

This is _____ the _____.

22.

This is _____ the _____.

23.

This is _____ the _____.

24.

This is _____ the _____.

25.

This is _____ the _____.

26.

This is _____ the _____.

KEYS TO EXERCISES

▶What's the first letter (1)

1. Yak; 2. Camel; 3. Kangaroo; 4. Tapir; 5. Bear; 6. Zebra

▶What's the first letter (2)

1. Jellyfish; 2. Iguana; 3. Rhino; 4. Viper; 5. Hippo; 6. Llama

▶What's the first letter (3)

1. Platypus; 2. Elephant; 3. Alligator; 4. Sloth; 5. Goat; 6. Wombat

▶What's the first letter (4)

1. Moose; 2. Dormouse; 3. Urchin; 4. Frog; 5. Otter; 6. Quail;
7. Numbat; 8. Lynx

▶Unscramble the letters (1)

1. ALLIGATOR; 2. ZEBRA; 3. WOMBAT; 4. YAK; 5. VIPER;
6. CAMEL

▶Unscramble the letters (2)

1. LLAMA; 2. HIPPO; 3. BEAR; 4. FROG; 5. RHINO; 6. KANGAROO

▶Unscramble the letters (3)

1. MOOSE; 2. GOAT; 3. ELEPHANT; 4. TAPIR; 5. SLOTH; 6. OTTER

▶Unscramble the letters (4)

1. IGUANA; 2. QUAIL; 3. URCHIN, 4. DORMOUSE; 5. NUMBAT;
6. JELLYFISH; 7. PLATYPUS; 8. LYNX

▶Connect the name to the animal (1)

1H / 2C / 3K / 4M / 5A / 6I / 7J / 8E / 9B / 10L / 11D / 12F / 13G

►Connect the name to the animal (2)

1I / 2F / 3K / 4J / 5M / 6L / 7B / 8D / 9G / 10A / 11H / 12C / 13E

►LISTEN AND WRITE THE NUMBER NEXT TO THE CORRESPONDING ANIMAL (1)

1. URCHIN; 2. FROG; 3. IGUANA; 4. NUMBAT; 5. MOOSE;
6. JELLYFISH; 7. OTTER; 8. HIPPO; 9. ALLIGATOR; 10. ZEBRA;
11. GOAT; 12. BEAR; 13. WOMBAT

►LISTEN AND WRITE THE NUMBER NEXT TO THE CORRESPONDING ANIMAL (2)

1. KANGAROO; 2. TAPIR; 3. QUAIL; 4. PLATYPUS; 5. SLOTH;
6. YAK; 7. ELEPHANT; 8. CAMEL; 9. LYNX; 10. DORMOUSE;
11. LLAMA; 12. RHINO; 13. VIPER

►Who are they?

1. This is Veronica the viper.
2. This is Jenny the jellyfish.
3. This is Suzy the sloth.
4. This is Eddy the elephant.
5. This is Neil the numbat.
6. This is Derek the dormouse.
7. This is Louis the llama.
8. This is Alfred the alligator.
9. This is Zoe the zebra.
10. This is Hector the hippo.
11. This is Claudia the camel.
12. This is Maurice the moose.
13. This is Irene the iguana.
14. This is Peter the platypus.
15. This is Willy the wombat.
16. This is Yanis the yak.
17. This is Queenie the quail.
18. This is Gina the goat.
19. This is Travis the tapir.
20. This is Olga the otter.

21. This is Kim the kangaroo.
22. This is Benny the bear.
23. This is Ricky the rhino.
24. This is Ursula the urchin.
25. This is Xena the lynx.
26. This is Fiona the frog.

Visit www.msieurthomas.com
to download the AUDIO PACK
containing all the tracks.

Use the code: ABC_pass87#
to unzip the files

Don't forget to check
My First Animal ABC video
on YouTube!

M'sieur Thomas

Thomas Gauthier

www.msieurthomas.com